From I Do to I Don't
Overcoming the Wounds of a Bad Relationship

Tricia-Anne Y. Morris

"…In all these things we overcome, because of Him that hath loved us." Romans 8:37 (DRA)

1

This book may be purchased for personal use from Amazon worldiwde. For speaking engagements, seminars, or workshops please write to:

> Tricia-Anne Y. Morris
> Anointed Words & Music, Inc.
> tricia.awminc@gmail.com

ISBN 978-976-95872-0-5

Published by Tricia-Anne Y. Morris.

DEDICATION

I dedicate this book to God, my Abba Father, my Redeemer, Source and Friend, my Everything, the I Am that I Am, who gives me wisdom. I thank You for birthing this book out of me. You could have chosen someone else but instead You chose me. I adore You, Lord.

I also dedicate this book to every woman and girl struggling in a bad, perhaps abusive, relationship or marriage.

ACKNOWLEDGEMENT

To my parents and siblings: I thank God for you always. You're wonderful, loving, constantly offering support. Dad, you inspire me with your writings. Mummy, you are a true woman of God and this causes me to want to please Him more. Dee, you're so brilliant, I look forward to your books. Kareem, your spiritual gifts are a light to those you encounter. Caryn, I love you dearly.

To Apostle Al Miller, senior pastor of my beloved Fellowship Tabernacle and president of Whole Life College, aka Bible School: I am very grateful to you. Sir, your sermons at church and lectures at Bible School empowered me and helped me in writing this book.

To everyone else who offered support during this journey, I am truly grateful.

FOREWORD

This wonderfully scripted work is nothing short of an act of bravery. Throughout its pages, Tricia-Anne Y. Morris has dared to bare her excoriated soul to the reader knowing full well that she has precious little control over where her story will go but hoping, no doubt, that by telling it in all its painful details, someone else will be spared the bitter heartache. It is Confucius who said:

By three methods we may gain wisdom:
First, by reflection, which is the noblest;
Second by imitation, which is the easiest; and
Third by experience, which is the bitterest.
(Paraphrased, Alfred Armand Montapert, 1986.)

In the pages that follow, Tricia-Anne provides ample opportunities for her readers to gain wisdom through reflection and through emulation. Emulation of the best choices she eventually makes because she chose to turn her own bitter experiences into opportunities for learning and spiritual growth.

The irony of the account disclosed so honestly and articulately in this work is that it is an oft repeated tale. One that is most often told in hushed tones and in secret places, passed on in confidence from one wounded soul to a dear friend, a mother, a confidant... less often to a pastor or a counselor. At other times it is chronicled in fables and novels, told in the third person so as to protect the identity of the affected persons. Seldom is there ever a first-person account that is so completely honest, soul-searchingly insightful, and to the point. This narrative speaks of her motives, her misgivings, her wishes and her oft-ignored better judgment. As we see the utterances of her secret voice emerge on the pages of the book, we recognize emotions with which we too have contended. We know the woman who lives within the pages of this book. We recognize her because we have lived with her.

Seldom do we have the courage to tell our stories out loud. Far more seldom is a writer able to give such a clear-eyed, heart-wrenching, honest account of what has transpired between two people in what has been an unhealthy courtship, marriage and, ultimately, the dissolution of a relationship.

What has resulted, in the case of Tricia-Anne's recounting of *From I Do to I Don't*, is a breath-taking page turner that you won't want to put down. In this work she has dared to give voice to her shortcomings, her insecurities, and her fears and has laid bare her soul for judgment by the unknown other.

Ms. Morris shares with us the thrill of setting out on her own as a young adult, the joy of meeting and spending time with new friends, the tentative excitement of a budding romance and the all-but-ignored warning "notes to self" that become recurrent themes in this story. All these elements provide momentum in the first chapters of the book. Her acknowledgement of the early signs of trouble that have gone unheeded or were rationalized away and, again, these "notes to self" so easily ignored, leads one to conclude that this relationship will not last the duration. Who then, will be the next suitor, and what could possibly happen to occupy the ensuing pages and chapters? One thing for sure, as we see this story unfold, this relationship won't last. This romance to which we have been introduced is headed for the rocks! As you keep reading – because you will not be able to stop (and while you're at it, remember to breathe) – you will discover that this story is not unfamiliar.

Interwoven within and throughout the work, is the heartwarming testimony of a young woman's journey to God to the realization of the unconditional, unrelenting and unceasing love of God. Again, Ms. Morris chronicles her journey with her characteristic eloquence and clarity. Like the account of the ill-advised relationship and all the less-than-wise choices that led to her misfortunes, her account is clear-eyed, matter-of-fact and unapologetic. Through these lenses, we are able to walk with the narrator through the fits and starts of the journey to God, to faith, and to spiritual fulfillment.

Without taking away from the bliss of love, the sanctity of marriage and the joy of bringing a new life into the world, Ms. Morris discloses the potential pitfalls of becoming entangled in unhealthy relationships and minimizing what should be glaring warning signs of a bad relationship. Apart from the verity of her own experience, she identifies some well documented behavioral signs that characterizes an abusive person and abusive relationships. However, she does not stop with the pathology of this bad relationship but goes on to chronicle her path out of despair and back to wholeness.

Many of us who read this book will attest to the credibility of its contents. Many of us will want to pass it on to the young (and not so young) people in our lives so that they may avoid some of the distress that often results from disregarding warning signs and thinking oneself the exception. We will choose to share with someone who is too afraid or too ashamed to get help or get out of an abusive relationship. It could be just the encouragement that someone needs to take a second look at his or her situation. Here is an opportunity to learn from "imitation" which is by far the easiest way of learning one of life's most critical lessons.

Be blessed,

V. Melody Bennett, Ph.D.
Stephen Minister

PREAMBLE

I've dedicated this book to God because He gave me the strength to overcome the trauma and disappointment of my relationship and later my marriage. I survived these experiences because of the relationship I now have with God as Husband, Father, Savior, Comforter and Friend. He heard my prayers in the wee hours of the morning and because He loves me, He replaced my sadness and pain with joy, laughter and dancing. He also gave me the strength to write this book.

I've also dedicated this book to you because I believe God wants you to know that you deserve better than the hurt, confusion and distress that you've been contending with. If you're in an abusive or tumultuous relationship, it isn't what He wants for you.

I wrote this book out of my own experience so it is primarily geared towards women. There is no intent, however, to belittle men because Scripture says *"the husband is the head of the wife as Christ is the head of the Church"* [Ephesians 5:23]. As there are good women in the world, there are also good men.

Nevertheless it must be strongly noted that abuse is wrong and no-one should accept it. It is never OK. You were adoringly and wonderfully made [Psalm 139:14] in the image and likeness of God [Genesis 1:26] which means He sees you as wonderful, beautiful and deserving of love.

God charges us to treat others as we would want to be treated [Matthew 7:12] and love each other as He has loved us [John 15:7]. It means then that He hates it when we don't love and hates it when we're not loved. It is never God's wish for us to accept the negative words that people say to us, to believe that we deserve to be treated badly even if it's by a loved one, or to think negatively about ourselves. He has given us affirmations and positive actions to use as our defense because He is perfection and so speaks and acts perfectly.

God intends for us to prosper. He wants us to prosper in every way - spiritually, emotionally, mentally, physically and financially [3 John 2]. God wants to make each of us His bride.

If you're going through or have been through this struggle and pain, give it up and take God's sweet love instead. Make Him the God of your life and circumstances. He alone can give you the answers you desire, the peace you need, and the joy to replace your sadness.

"The Lord your God is with you, the Mighty Warrior who saves. He will take delight in you; in His love He will no longer rebuke you, but will rejoice over you with singing" [Zephaniah 3:17].

Every blessing,

Tricia-Anne Y. Morris

TABLE OF CONTENTS

ADVISORY

The information and suggestions provided in this book are not intended to take the place of sound spiritual and professional advice, whether counseling, medical advice or otherwise. Readers are advised to consult with a pastor, physician, therapist or other professional practitioner where necessary. The author and publisher do not assume any liability for possible adverse consequences as a result of the information contained herein.

Names, identifying details and locales have been changed to protect the privacy of individuals.

PART I
TALES FROM A NIGHTMARISH RELATIONSHIP

If you can relate to any part of the story written in the next few chapters, you may need to ask yourself if you're in the right relationship. My hope is that you'll evaluate your relationship, and if you've determined you need help you'll find the strength to either pray your way through to a turnaround or walk away, in Jesus' name.

CHAPTER 1

I was excited about moving into my new apartment. I had waited a year for it. It was a rental but I was excited because I needed to move out of my mother's home. Needed my own space for no other reason but that I believed it was time. Thirty-five, single, and living at home was not a good look for me. *(That was the first lie I told myself. My mom and I had a wonderful relationship. I had my own space at home which I loved. I really had no reason to move.)*

I fell in love with the place the moment I saw it. It was a huge one bedroom apartment painted in warm spring colors with a balcony overlooking a lush green lawn and a second floor view of the mountainside. I didn't have the money to take it at that time. So I told my colleague about it. She took it. I was disappointed but stayed hopeful that something affordable would come along soon.

It was a year before something came up. I screamed so hard when she told me. She had decided to buy her own place and so would move out of mine. On top of that God's timing was perfect. I actually had the money to take it now.

Wow, finally my own place. Thank You, Lord.

~

He lived in the apartment next door but didn't live alone. They popped in to see me for short visits, sometimes together, other times it would just be him. *(Mistake: Don't spend time alone with a man who is not your husband. Spending time alone may lead to sex. Sex only clouds things. Of course, you will never truly know if this relationship you want so much is built on a strong foundation or just sex. Spending time alone can also lead to sexual assault or rape. When courting, do group dates instead.)*

One night he told their story. She was his best friend. They had dated for a few years but when it didn't work out they remained roommates. He had lost his job two years before and was now broke. So she took care of him. He depended on her for everything. *(Caution: A man who has to depend on a woman for a protracted period may become aggressive towards her as he tries to cope with the insecurities and feelings of inadequacy that may emerge.)*

I mulled over the story and decided that he clearly thought I was an idiot. Who would buy that story'? A man living with a woman that he wasn't intimate with was too ridiculous to be true. However, a few days later she and I were chatting and she told me the same thing. She also said it was clear that we liked each other so we should go for it.

What! I didn't like him. What gave her that impression? Did I like him? True, he was pretty cool and we got along well. Anyway, I wouldn't date a man who was living with another woman. That was out of the question. I wasn't a Christian but I had Christian values.

~

I came home one day from work and he was no longer living next door. He had moved out because he felt it was an unhealthy situation. All of a sudden I found myself thinking that we could actually start dating. I even started fantasizing about what that would be like.

He still came by the apartment complex. He had moved back home with his parents and though he now lived farther away, he didn't mind coming over to see us because he really had no friends where his mom and dad lived.

Like before, they both popped in but more and more it was only him. Before long I came to the conclusion that there was really nothing stopping us from dating. *(That was the second lie I told myself: I didn't really know him as we had only spent time chit-chatting. Chit-chatting with somebody doesn't equal knowing them. Not knowing each other may result in conflict and discomfort in the long run. Spend time doing different things together on your group dates. It's important to see how he operates in different situations so you get a sense of what he is like and what he likes.)*

~

We started dating but felt it best to keep the relationship under wraps. Well, I did. It felt weird to me that I had just moved in a couple of months ago, just met this guy who used to live with the girl next door and now we were dating. *(Mistake: If you have to hide your relationship it may not be of God: "He knows what lies in darkness, and light dwells with Him" [Daniel 2:22])*

To keep it under wraps, even from her, we included her when we hung out. All this, so nobody would become suspicious. I had to admit though that it got a little tricky when we hung out with his family or friends.

One day the three of us hung out. He asked a question. She answered. Then out of nowhere came this rage as he cursed at her, told her she was stupid, and then told her to shut up. *(Alarm bells: Take note of how a man treats others, including his parents, children, and especially, other women. It's a good indication of what kind of man he is and how he will treat you. A man cursing, physically or emotionally abusing and/or disrespecting you raises serious questions about the quality of the love he has for you.)*

I noticed he constantly spoke to her like that. He was also like that with some of his male friends who would back off once his posture changed. In fact, more and more I noticed that he would shout or swear at people, and be oversensitive to what was being said. *(Mistake: These behaviors should have alerted me to the dangers. I should have realized that he was aggressive, insecure and had a bad temper. Research has identified common signals of aggression. These include clenched fists/teeth/jaws, staring eyes, swearing, verbal abuse, standing too close, banging/kicking things, stomping feet, loud speech or shouting, pointing or jabbing with the finger, and an aggressive posture and/or tone of voice.[1])*

I guess some persons would argue that words don't harm. However, I would disagree, which is why I made sure to tell him how wrong he was to have treated her like that. I was determined to stand up for her. I wanted to champion her cause and the cause of so many women who had no voice because they were so scared of the men they were dating, or had such low self-esteem that they didn't realize when a man was trampling all over them. I felt good knowing I stood up to him for her sake. That way he would also know never to try that with me. *(Third lie: Standing up for her was not the same as telling him that I wouldn't accept his abuse.)*

---

[1] How to Recognise Aggression. Accessed at
http://www.skillsyouneed.com/ps/dealing-with-aggression2.html

20

~

I heard them next door arguing again. His phone accidentally dialed my number. He was swearing at her. This time an object was used and she got hit in the face. His side of the story was that she threw something at him and he threw it back but didn't mean to hit her. *(Alarm bells: A man or woman who lacks self-control isn't yet ready for marriage. To throw something at someone else is an indication of a lack of self-control, whether or not the intent was to hit the person.)*

I couldn't believe it. What kind of man hits a woman?

~

Although I saw the signs I ignored them. Isn't that funny? Strange even? I grew up having in mind what a man should be like and should not be like. I was fully aware of what to look for and run away from. I even went as far as to declare to my mother, on occasion, that if he even seemed a little bit weird I'd be out the door. Yet I ignored the signs and continued to date this man. I guess in the back of my mind I had decided that he would never do the same to me.

CHAPTER 2

Five months into the relationship and he had asked me to marry him. I was so ecstatic. I had always wanted to be married. Plus, it felt good knowing that we hadn't been dating long and already he was asking me to be his wife. *(Mistake: A marriage proposal does not validate you as a woman. It doesn't qualify you for some grand prize. Whether you marry or not, you should live your life knowing that YOU are adoringly and wonderfully made [Psalm 139:14]. That is what validates you. I still believe that marriage is a wonderful institution. However, I also believe that it only helps our marriage if we accept who God says we are, that we are loved by him and deserving of love by our spouse. Not accepting will negatively affect our marriage and other relationships.)*

I immediately thought to myself - no more premarital affairs, no more wondering when my turn will come, no more longing for children. I would finally be able to settle down and live happily ever after. Suddenly, somewhere in the heat of the excitement I found myself asking - Did he want children though? What were his views on marriage? What about the fact that he didn't have a job, how did he intend to care for our family? What about finances? I was sure to make more money than him even if he did get a job – how would he feel about that and how would that affect our relationship? Did he manage money well? Where did he see himself in five years?

Whoa…I realized I needed to slow it down because I really didn't know anything about this man and his vision in relation to marriage, children or life on a whole. *(Caution: Don't assume you share the same vision. If your visions are not moving in the same direction you will have conflicts. This suggests you may be rushing things or choosing the wrong relationship. Your core beliefs, values, goals, and interests should coincide. Ask critical questions upfront.)*

Why did he want to marry me anyway? Yes we felt we loved each other, but what were we measuring that against? How did we know for sure that we loved each other? What if this was just lust? What if I was rushing into this because I really just wanted to be married? *(Fact: Lust and attraction are not love. Lust and attraction will fade as time passes, especially if the relationship faces challenges. Some women reading this may say that won't happen to them because they know for sure that they're in love, but what if it happens to him? What if he realizes he's not in love with you?)*

I decided since my dad was coming for a visit I would see if he approved, after which I would make up my mind.

~

Daddy had a funeral to attend outside of the city and he was taking us along for the ride. His intent of course was to see how this man treated me. This short two hour drive wasn't sufficient time to determine whether or not he would meet his approval but it was certainly a start.

Daddy saw what I saw; the loving side of this man, who cooked for me, served me, stayed up at night when I had to study and touched me tenderly just because. *(Fact: People are very capable of being gentle and loving in one instance and aggressive and bullish in another. We should stop telling ourselves that the aggressive times are just a fluke. That side may very well be more real than the loving, tender side. I believe we should be open to forgiving someone when they make such a mistake. However, there is a point at which we may*

23

need to just walk away if the situation is harmful and over time things do not improve.)

We stopped at a restaurant along the way. My dad watched as he pulled out my chair for me, took my meal and placed it on the table before me, took wipes and gently cleaned my hands and then whisked my garbage away once I was done eating. These were the kind of things men were expected to do, and for my dad it was great to see a man actually do them for his daughter.

We chatted on the way back into the city. He asked my dad questions about marriage. Some of his questions made for good conversation. It was generally a good day.

After a few more days with us daddy gave a nod. OK, not so much a nod, but he did say he liked him. Of course, I ran with that. I mean, that was enough, right? *(Lie: In my desperation for marriage I convinced myself that if daddy liked him, then it was a 'yes' but how could daddy truly have known him after a few hours, especially when he was on his best behavior; trying to impress.)*

Daddy liked him and God allowed us to meet. He must have since He got me the apartment. Since there were no coincidences with God He must have brought us together. *(Mistake: Avoid using 'signs' as your only guide when making a life changing decision. The truth is, when you want something badly 'signs' tend to conveniently agree with whatever you want to hear. That's because you usually have blinders on and wouldn't see the red flags even if they were screaming at you. Instead, spend time planning, evaluating and praying. Look at the pros and cons and don't move until you've sought wise counsel and finally have peace about it.)*

~

After his proposal I started feeling safe about telling people that we had been dating for a while and had decided to get married. It was no surprise to most people as they all had noticed that I was beaming. According to them, it was obvious I was happy and in love. *(Fact: People often talk about being in love based on the mushy emotions they feel for someone. These emotions are not enough to sustain a marriage. They can't feed you, put a roof over your heads or pay the bills. They certainly can't guarantee your faithfulness and commitment to one another. What will sustain you and your marriage is building your foundation on Jesus Christ: "and the one who trusts in Him shall never be put to shame" [1 Peter 2:6]. Mushy is good but shouldn't be your only reason for moving forward.)*

We started making plans for the wedding. We did everything together. We checked a few hotels and possible locations to have the wedding. We sampled food from a few restaurants and caterers. We looked at wedding colors. We decided on a theme. We even looked at rings, did some fittings and made plans for the honeymoon. Yet we made very few plans for after the wedding. It was when we went to counselling that we realized there was much to discuss regarding after the wedding but we never got around to it. *(Mistake: Be careful not to get caught up in the euphoria of the wedding without also considering after the wedding, because the wedding is not the marriage. You need a plan for after the wedding. In fact not making plans for the future is a recipe for disaster. Planning is critical because it helps to give you direction. Premarital counselling is very useful. It helps you to plan and consider things you may not agree on as well as how to handle these disagreements.)*

~

It didn't matter to either of us that our parents were apprehensive. It didn't matter that my mom kept asking if this was the right decision to make. It didn't matter that his parents didn't like me or that my mother was wary of him. All that mattered was that we were getting married. *(Mistake: If the people that are closest to you, those you trust most, raise a red flag, step back and reevaluate. It's a strong indication that something could be wrong. Marriage is a lifelong commitment, a huge decision. Make sure your loved ones are on board before moving ahead. They usually see things you don't. The truth is he should ask permission for your hand in marriage as a courtesy to your parents/guardians. If they don't readily approve then maybe you need to take a more serious look at your relationship. Again, doing counseling before committing to a final decision may help in these instances.)*

~

We agreed that we would save for the wedding and our new life. So I moved back home to my mom. We also decided on buying a car. We looked into it and hiring a taxicab to get around cost just as much as having a car. So the car made more sense. Plus, he had a job now which meant we could stretch for the car.

Since he hadn't been working a long while, he wasn't eligible for a loan. That meant I had to take out the loan for the car myself. My credit was good so getting the loan was easy. Once we collected the cash from the bank we sorted out all the paper work for the car. Because we were going to be married I registered the car in both our names. *(Mistake: Until you say "I do" you're not married. Buying a car, house or any other major item or property with someone ties you to that person. Getting out of that kind of situation may be difficult. Putting someone's name on your mortgage or car papers means that person becomes legally entitled to monies from the sale. Be absolutely sure this is the best move for you before you make such a huge commitment.)*

He wasn't making a lot of money at his new job so we agreed that I would make the monthly payments on the loan while he would be responsible for filling the gas tank each week and for servicing the car as needed.

CHAPTER 3

He picked me up for work every morning. It was great. We were able to spend time together on our commute back and forth. We even hung out after work at my mom's for a while in the evenings before he headed back to his parents' place. Every now and again we'd even take a drive up into the hills and enjoy the scenery and beautiful mansions. We would also go out to the countryside for the weekend. It was hard not being able to spend more time together but we had to keep within budget if we wanted to be married later that year.

~

Was I imaging things? Was something wrong with this picture or was I making too much of it? Two months ago we had a great routine. However these days he would be late in picking me up, making me late for work. He rarely stayed behind anymore after we got home to my mom's. The gas tank was always on empty and more and more I had to be filling it up. He was going out with his friends from work most weekends now to these 'staff-only parties'. On top of all that, it seemed the excitement of planning our wedding had worn off for him.

He was behaving strangely. He said it was because he felt pressured like I was rushing things. I wasn't sure how he moved from being excited about the wedding to acting weird. However, my friends suggested that I slow it down a bit. They felt I was rushing things.

OK but it still didn't explain the issues we were having with money and why last month he asked me for money to help a relative out of a difficult situation. All of this left me with hardly any savings and made it difficult for me to make the car payments.

I contemplated whether to postpone the wedding but opted not to. Instead I took my friends' advice and slowed things down. I figured that would get things back to normal.

~

He got weirder day by day. Everything about the wedding was now a problem. It was like he constantly wanted to pick a fight and every time we fought he would disappear for days.

It got even worse. We not only fought about the wedding. We fought about everything. I guess after what happened with his ex-girlfriend I shouldn't have been surprised when he turned on me with the same kind of disrespect and rage. Yet I was blown out of the water.

We were chatting and I disagreed with something he said. I was shocked because in my mind we weren't even arguing. However, as he blew up, flashbacks of similar situations with others, including his ex, came to mind. I realized after a while that he hated when people disagreed with him.

That kind of argument became an almost everyday occurrence. It felt like I wasn't supposed to have my own opinion on anything. When I tried to talk to him about it he turned it around on me by saying I was trying to make him feel like he didn't matter, that I clearly didn't think he was smart enough. *(Fact: A man that constantly responds with aggression when you disagree with him is either suffering from rejection or low self-esteem, or is a control freak. He may respond in fits of rage because in his mind whatever you say or do suggests to him that he's of little worth. He then blames you to feel better about himself but really what he needs is help. Spend time praying for him. Pray also that he seeks help on a spiritual and emotional level. Until he gets help you're likely to continue to be the target of his abusive behavior.)*

OK. Not sure how we got here but since I believed in 'picking my battles' I was determined to try to find another way to say things. If it wasn't something critical I just went along with him and allowed him to speak, but we ended up arguing just the same because he felt I was patronizing him. I tried other tactics thinking they would calm him down but nothing worked.

His words were really very painful and I would cry myself to sleep sometimes just thinking about them. What made it worse was that I wasn't accustomed to this type of treatment. I had always enjoyed loving relationships. Yet this man swore at me, told me I was stupid and threatened to kill me. On top of that he hardly said "I love you" or complimented me anymore. He would even criticize me, and criticize anyone that said kind things to or about me. Friends also told me that he spoke disparagingly about me when I wasn't around. I had never liked gossip, so I would ignore whatever they had to say rather than recognize it as them alerting me.

~

With all of that I still didn't walk away. I guess because we had only exchanged words and nothing physical happened. I mean, we were getting married so it should change, right?

(Another lie – This one is so common among us women. How a person is before marriage is an indication of how that person will be during marriage. Don't go into marriage thinking you'll change the other person. Try to discuss and work through these things before. Situations like these require intervention. Spend time praying about it and get professional help. Importantly, if things aren't changing over time, be honest with yourself and walk away if that's your best or only option.)

Maybe I came into this with some preconceived notions about love and relationships. Maybe we're having these issues because, like they say, men and women are from two different worlds and we find it hard to communicate because we talk, think and behave differently. If that's true then we can fix this.

I decided to get advice from my friend Erik. Erik was a manly man, engaged to a wonderful woman who had her head on straight. They were a solid couple. Yes, like everyone else they had had their own struggles but I quite liked the fact that they were able to get over them with good Christian counselling and a strong commitment to each other. I also trusted Erik. He was honest and real so I knew he would tell me like it was. Plus he was a man. He would better appreciate what another man was thinking or feeling.

Who best to talk to than someone that was acquainted with the two of us? I had introduced them some time ago and they had hit it off. They had similar ideas regarding business and were even talking about partnering to take on some ventures together. So I figured since he knew us both he could give a more objective perspective.

Erik and I met over lunch. I poured my heart out. I

explained that when it was good it was amazing but when it was bad it was horrible and unfortunately there were a lot more bad times than good times. I didn't pretty anything up. I even mentioned mistakes I had made and situations I had handled poorly. I wanted everything out in the open because I wanted to be sure that the advice I got was based on sound reasoning.

Erik didn't beat around the bush. He went straight for the jugular. Bottom line, he didn't like what my man was up to. As far as he was concerned this man was not ready for a commitment but didn't know it and this made him the worst kind of man to date. The kind that would beat his chest saying 'I'm a man, I'm an adult and I know what I'm doing' when none of the above applied. He told me to pack it in because staying would just bring me more distress and pain. Purely because a man like mine wasn't looking to change. He wasn't looking to be a better man for anybody, much less for himself.

After that talk with Erik I decided it was time to walk away.

CHAPTER 4

Are you serious! I had finally made up my mind to leave yet here I was learning that I was pregnant. I thought it must have been a joke. It must have been punishment for dating this man in the first place. It felt like a bad dream. I was in shock because I knew I would now be stuck with him for the rest of my life.

What did I expect? I had stopped taking contraceptives without telling him weeks ago because I thought if I got pregnant things would get better. *(Mistake: Trapping a man with pregnancy is never a good idea. The decision to have a child should be handled responsibly. The couple should agree together that this is what they both want. Too many children suffer from rejection and abandonment. Remember, the man may just stay because he feels he has no choice and so may not bring the kind of love or joy to fatherhood that a child deserves. Likewise, the man may leave, causing the child to grow up fatherless. Bear in mind what Scripture says about the bad decisions we make surrounding children: "If anyone causes one of these little ones—those who believe in me—to stumble, it would be better for them if a large millstone were hung around their neck and they were thrown into the sea" [Mark 9:42])*

~

Fast forward. The idea of being a mom made me very happy. It no longer mattered that it was his baby. I was pregnant. I loved children and had wanted a child for years now. In any event, maybe this could bring the turnaround in our relationship that I had been longing for.

He said he was excited and it was the best gift anyone could have ever given him but his eyes told a different story. I ignored it though, expecting this to mark a new day in our relationship. I was very hopeful.

~

For weeks things were great. We were arguing less and were actually making plans for the future. We were spending more time together and meeting up at lunch time since our offices were close to each other. We mostly shared my lunch because he didn't have enough money to buy his own and my funds were low from having to spend more on food, prenatal medication and seeing the obstetrician. *(Fact: Like marriage, pregnancy should be well thought out and planned for. It costs to be pregnant, give birth and raise a child. Don't step into it without first ensuring that you can afford it financially, emotionally, physically and mentally.)*

Then came the roller-coaster ride. I hated it. We were good; getting along better. Things were looking up, but just a month in and everything changed for the worse. He had gone back to cursing and behaving like a monster. We were arguing more than ever before. I felt like I was in a war zone. I could actually feel my belly griping from the distress. He never had a kind word; always something negative.

I was also stressed out about our money problems. He had stopped giving me money all together. He even stopped putting gas in the car. Money was so tight that I sometimes didn't have enough for lunch. I was scared this was affecting the baby; it wasn't healthy for either of us. I just knew she was under a lot of pressure. *(Fact: Babies who suffer emotional stress during pregnancy are likely to suffer developmental and/or neurological disorders such as anxiety, ADHD, and autism spectrum disorder.)*[2]

~

One day I saw a colleague of his from work who said something strange. She told me that as far as she was concerned I was the best 'wife' he had ever had and none of the others could compare. I found it strange because as far as I knew she didn't know any of his exes. She barely knew him because he had only started working there a few months before.

Was she inadvertently telling me that my man was seeing someone else? I couldn't get it out of my mind. As I thought about it I realized she gave me a look that said *I won't be the one to come straight out and say it so I hope you get my drift.*

I got to work the next day and a colleague of mine said that she had seen him at the movies with another woman and her child. How could he go to the movies without me? Why didn't he tell me he was going?

A little later I got a call from a friend who said she had seen him with another woman in our car. My instinct told me right away that it was her. He had the woman he was cheating with in my car. The car I bought and was still paying for.

While I was still contemplating how to handle all this, he

[2] Alice Walton (2012). How Parent's Stress Can Hurt a Child from the Inside Out. Accessed at www.forbes.com.

called to say he couldn't make it for lunch because his supervisor asked him to take the lunch shift. I wanted to scream at him because I was so mad, but I didn't have it in me. I just said OK and hung up. I needed time to think, to calm down. I went into my boss' office since he wasn't at work that day. I stared out the window for a while. I was numb. Then I saw them walking from behind some building. They worked together.

Now it all made sense. Whenever I called his parents' house early in the morning his mother would say he's not there. One morning she even suggested that he hadn't slept at home but then quickly changed the subject. My friends had even seen him coming from another direction rather than that of his parent's house when he was supposed to be on his way in the mornings to pick me up.

I spent the rest of the day recounting that image I had of them walking side by side. After work we walked down to pick up the car from the parking garage. I asked him about her. He said she was just a friend. I knew he was lying but when I thought about it I also knew that the evidence I had was all circumstantial.

Nevertheless, I decided to take the car because I didn't want any other woman in it. I refused to be spending my money on a car to entertain him and some other girl. So I made plans to go jogging with a girlfriend of mine in the evenings after work. He was mad and yelling, behaving as though he was entitled to the car and that I had no right to ask for it. I ignored him and decided I was keeping the car no matter what. In fact, I had made up my mind to sell it with or without him.

I dropped him home before going for my jog. He slammed the car door and told me never to come back to his parents' house, all while calling me derogatory names. I thanked God that I never had to see him again.

~

Two weeks went by. We were back together because I didn't want my child to grow up without a father. I didn't feel the same way about him as I did before but decided to stick it out for the baby's sake. I knew it would be hard but I thought it best to put my baby's needs before my own.

CHAPTER 5

He took the car and headed out of town very early one Saturday morning to spend the day by his friend's farm. He explained that the terrain on the farm would be too much for me so it wasn't a good idea for me to go. So I stayed home. We spoke throughout the day. He even sent pictures of the farm. He was really having a great time.

My friends called to say they were coming to get me at 8:30 p.m. to go play board games. As was customary, we bought food and set up to play until the wee hours of the morning. They asked how things were going. I explained that things weren't going well, though I decided to stay for the baby's sake.

We played for a few hours. Then I noticed at 11 p.m. that I hadn't heard from him for a while. I figured it was because of the poor mobile coverage in the area, so I waited a bit longer before trying to call him again. At 1 a.m. I still hadn't heard from him. I started to get anxious. I thought maybe something bad had happened. Images of the car falling over a cliff somewhere popped into my mind. I was so scared that my friends and I got into their car to drive by his mom's house to see if he had gotten in OK. The car wasn't there. I became terrified.

At 4 a.m. I finally got through to him. He told me mobile coverage was weak and so his calls wouldn't go through. He said he got in after 11 p.m. and went straight home to his mom's house but didn't bother to stop by mine because he thought I would be sleeping.

Did he just say that he got back home by 11 p.m.? How is that possible? The car wasn't there when we stopped by? So I asked him what had happened to the car. He responded saying "it was fine. It was outside where it's always parked".

I couldn't sleep after we spoke because I knew he was lying. At 7 a.m. I called my friend Brian and asked him to go check if the car was parked at the house. Brian called to confirm that the car wasn't there. Since Brian lived nearby he made a second trip at 9 a.m. Still no car.

At about 10:30am I heard our car pull up to my mom's gate. He came in smiling, excited about the visit to the farm. I listened but he noticed after a while that I wasn't saying much and that I wasn't excited for him. I told him I knew he was lying about the night before. He started to speak but I stopped him in his tracks, calmly asking where he wanted me to leave him because I was through with the relationship. He started shouting. I calmly asked again if there was anywhere in particular he needed me to leave him.

The nerve of him; he started cursing in my mother's home. He knew my mother wouldn't approve of that kind of behavior. What would possess him to do such a thing? I told him he had to leave. He shouted louder. I threatened to call the police.

He went towards the front door. I walked behind him without saying a word. I was happy to open the door to let him out. However he spun around and threw me on the couch and tried hitting me in my stomach. I screamed and hit him in the face.

My neighbor had heard us arguing and ran over. She screamed at him in shock when she saw him reaching for my stomach with his fists. He got up and started to walk behind me as I headed to the kitchen for a knife to defend myself. My neighbor warned him and told him to leave. She told him if he didn't leave she would call the men from the neighborhood. He walked out. As he did so he remarked that he was tired of me taking risks with his baby. *(Fact: When they get caught men who abuse women will tell lies to cover their tracks.)*

Days and weeks passed and I refused to take his call. He was banned from my mother's home and I wanted him out of my life.

~

I finally took his call after a friend of his visited and told me that he wasn't handling the break up well and said if I didn't give him another chance he would commit suicide. *(Fact: Men who abuse women sometimes use suicide to manipulate the women into staying. They often have no intention of committing suicide but know that the woman is likely to feel guilty and succumb to manipulation.)*

On our first call he was barking and telling me it's my fault he cheated because I was controlling and always spoke to him in a condescending manner. I hung up, refusing to continue our conversation with him shouting at me.

He called the following day and started shouting again. I made it clear that I would only stay on the phone if he stopped. He calmed down and said once more that it was my fault he cheated. He told me again that I was controlling and condescending. Controlling because I would ask him about how he was spending money, including my money, and condescending because I would use big words just to make him feel small. I was dumbfounded. I could not believe that was the best he could come up with. He must have been losing his mind. The wedding was off.

~

It was a week before we spoke again. He called to apologize. He came clean about the affair, about staying over by her house after leaving the farm, and apologized for everything, including attacking me. This time, however, he said that he was now ready to be a man and father. He now realized that I meant more to him than she ever would and she was just a fling. I stared at the phone thinking "I really don't care but good to know you'll at least try to be a father to our child". I told him I would think about it.

He called every day for the next couple of weeks. I barely spoke.

~

I picked him up so we could talk. He was the father of my child and I realized that I could not avoid him for much longer. He told me he wanted us to try again. He also promised never to speak to her again. Yet he wanted to be a father to her son. According to him, she was not much of a mother. He said the child's father was no better.

I listened. I pulled up at his mother's gate. He asked me if I wanted to come in. I said no. He started to get out the car. I turned towards him, laughed and sped away.

~

Our relationship had come to a standstill, though I'm not sure he realized it. He kept talking about the future while all I could think of was how much of a mistake it was to be pregnant for him. If only there was a way out.

I thought, "Perhaps tomorrow when I wake up he'll be gone. Maybe they'll run off together". It's not like he hadn't thought of it before. I recalled seeing his emails to her about moving to Canada and taking her with him. He had asked me to give him the money to go but I didn't have the money at the time.

Even if there was a way to get that money I wouldn't have given it to him. I knew he was lying about having a job there – some friend with a restaurant. I didn't believe a word. He even tried to convince me that he would have sent a ticket for me to visit once he got settled and had enough money. He didn't know that I had seen the emails where he had told her the same thing. Anyway I probably should have said yes. At least I would have been rid of all this by now. *(Caution: If the relationship isn't working after much effort and counseling you should consider whether it's time to walk away. A talk show host said 'if the man is emotionally and/or physically abusing you and you decide to stay you're no longer the victim. You've become the perpetrator. You're the one victimizing yourself.' Perhaps there is some truth to that.)*

CHAPTER 6

It was 9 p.m. I was feeling discomfort and was spotting. I called my doctor. She assured me there was nothing to worry about but my friend from school who was also pregnant suggested that I go to the Emergency Room.

I called to tell him that I needed to go to the hospital. He had no money to put gas in the car so he couldn't pick me up.

I found my way to the hospital. They rushed me into surgery. They explained that I was going into premature labor.

He got money from a friend to buy gas for the car and made it to the hospital just in time to see me before they took me in for surgery. He promised to do better. He told me that he would rather lose the baby than lose me. I smiled. There's something about trauma and tragedy that brings people closer together. That something made me feel inclined to give it another try. So we made a new commitment to each other and agreed that no matter the outcome we would make our relationship work.

I was almost 6 months pregnant. It was a girl. She didn't make it.

~

He had taken quite a bit of money from my bank account. I guess I should never have given him my debit card. I gave it to him months ago when we decided to get married. Problem is, he was poor at handling money. He was one of those persons who believed in spending big and worrying about the consequences later. I was quite the opposite. I had school loans, a car loan and paid bills at my mom's home, so I didn't have the luxury of binge spending.

I had been in the hospital and hadn't checked my bank account in quite a while. So now that I was back online I noticed that he not only took a lot of money but he used the card for all sorts of things. I asked him about it. He said he needed a few things and needed money for gas because it was expensive travelling back and forth to the hospital every day. That didn't make sense to me based on the amount he had taken.

~

I almost didn't see it. But there it was. He had used my card at a motel. I was livid. I went to see him at his parent's house demanding that he give me back my debit card. He threw my card to the ground. I couldn't find it anywhere. I finally stepped out of the house and drove off. On my way home I called the bank and cancelled the card. I went in the next day to get a new one.

I was in the hospital recovering from the death of his child. Yet all he could think about was spending time with this woman. He spent my money and used my car so he could be with her. I couldn't help but think that losing the baby was a blessing in disguise. I realized that I needed this man out of my life for good.

~

He called me to say he was sorry. He said he wanted to tell me the whole truth. The woman he had the affair with got in trouble and he felt compelled to help because of her son. So he borrowed the money from my account to help out. He promised to find a way to pay me back.

I went back and forth in my mind about this money. However, I realized that I was more upset about this connection he had with her than I was about him spending the money. What was it about her and her son that made him feel he needed to protect them?

I felt betrayed by him. I felt really hurt. It got so bad I didn't even want to hear his name.

~

Dealing with the loss of my child was more difficult than I had bargained for. I would cry and scream a lot. I would have suicidal thoughts.

I was back at work but I couldn't think straight. My family had been very supportive but I was feeling depressed and physically ill.

I had finally decided that I needed to be with him. I had convinced myself that he was the only one who would really understand what I was going through because it happened to him too. *(Mistake: Getting back together with someone after such a traumatic event may not be a good idea. It is sometimes quite like starting a relationship on the rebound. You're not thinking clearly, you're emotionally unstable and are unable to make sound decisions. It's likely to turn out badly. Take time to evaluate your feelings, and whether getting back together is a good decision for you. If it doesn't feel right, if you still have concerns, then step back and take more time to decide your next move. Praying and journalizing are usually very helpful in these situations.)*

~

I had been at work feeling despondent over the loss of my child. I felt overwhelmed. My mobile phone rang. I was told my uncle had just died. I felt like the pain was being compounded. It felt like what I suspect a nervous breakdown would feel like. A few weeks later my teenage sister had a stroke. It was too much for me. I didn't know God the way I do now so all I could think was, "though being with him was hard, I needed this man to help me through this heartache". *(Fact: Human beings will disappoint you because just like you they are far from perfect. There are those that need healing just as much as you do. Some need healing from past aches and disappointments. Many are going through struggles even now. But God who is Healer, Deliverer, Friend, Father and Way Maker is perfect and so, He, and He alone, can offer you the peace you so desire.)*

Why was I so drawn to this man? This man who had disrespected me, lied to me, stolen from me, cheated on me, and had emotionally, verbally, and physically abused me. Why wasn't I convinced that I needed to walk away? True he's a good looking guy who sometimes did nice things but the bad far outweighed the good.

Why was I behaving like he was the only man who had ever shown an interest in me? I had been in greater relationships with more well-adjusted men who had lots more going for them. Plus, I'm a good looking woman, well-educated, great personality even with my flaws, good career, assertive, well-accomplished. I deserved better than this. Yet my inner strength didn't seem to want to kick in and give me the boost I needed to finally be done with this relationship. *(Fact: Many of us have had to deal with offences, anger, shame, disappointments, depression, guilt, unforgiveness, trauma or heart break, and these often result in emotional wounds. Also, the wounds we carry are sometimes generational. Somewhere in the family tree there's a wound or wounds that never got closed and so the cycle continues with us. I think for me it was my parent's divorce, seeing my relative struggle with mental illness, being molested as a child and later in adulthood by a friend, the negative words from my relationship and the womanizing that started with my great grandfather. Ignoring the wounds caused them to deepen. The deeper they got the more I opened up myself to fear, rejection and low self-esteem. Women who struggle with fear, rejection and low self-esteem at some point may get pulled into an abusive relationship.)*

~

God, I was giving this man one more chance.

CHAPTER 7

We had started over. We decided to rent somewhere together. I wasn't comfortable with it because I didn't believe in shacking up with a man, but went along with it because I thought I needed him to help me get over the loss of our baby. It didn't matter that the baby was gone, that he had lost his job and that my feelings for him had changed. It didn't even matter that the financial burden of living together would be all on me. I just needed to heal and he was all I thought I could lean on.

We searched all over and finally found a place we both really liked. However, we couldn't afford it and so continued looking at other places. The other places we had seen turned out to be more expensive, smaller and pretty much uninhabitable. As we were about to give up on our search I got a call from a company I had applied to. The job was mine. We could finally take the place we both had set our hearts on.

~

I suggested we sell the car and use the money from the sale to clear the back payments on the car loan, buy furniture for the apartment, make a payment towards my outstanding school fee and put the rest down for groceries and rent for the months to come. He didn't want to sell the car and suggested I borrow the money from the bank or from my dad instead. I said no. See, here's the issue. A man should take care of his responsibilities. Instead he abused his. He had his other woman in the car I bought and struggled to pay for. Struggled to pay for because he chose to spend his money on her rather than put gas in the car or take care of any other financial commitments he had, leaving me to bear the burden. My mind was made up. I didn't care how upset he was. I would sell the car and he would just have to get over it.

~

He moved into the apartment two days before I did because someone needed to be there when the furniture delivery man came. He had lost his job because of insubordination. It was his third strike. I guess it all worked out because it meant he was able to meet the delivery man during work hours. Something I wasn't able to do.

When I finally moved in he had cleaned the place, unpacked everything and cooked dinner. We chatted for hours. It was a good start to a new life. In fact, the first two or so months were great. We got along well, and though I didn't feel as committed as I did before, I was determined to give it a try.

~

It was the weekend. I had decided to do some washing. He stood outside while I hung the clothes out. I had finished putting everything out on the line when he decided to walk behind me and rehang them. He said I hadn't done it properly.

Rather than argue I went along with the flow and left for the kitchen to make one of his favorite meals. He had always said he enjoyed my cooking. So naturally I was surprised when he walked behind me to re-season my pot and adjust the burners, then give me 'advice' on how to cook this dish that I had cooked with great success long before I even met him. I smiled and left him to finish up. Like I said before, 'I pick my battles'.

The following day I got up very early as I had decided the night before to do more laundry. As I sorted the clothes, he started to point out that I was doing it all wrong. He then decided to take over all the household chores because, according to him, I had no clue what I was doing. Fact is, he found fault with everything I did; the way I spoke, every opinion I had, the way I did chores, everything.

~

My dad and step mom decided to visit for their anniversary. I invited them to stay at the apartment as we both agreed we wanted to have them over. My dad declined. I should have expected it though. Daddy was hugely disappointed in him. Of course, neither of my parents was happy that I stayed with him after he attacked me. They were even more upset that I had decided to move in with him.

I wanted things to be right with my parents and wanted us to start afresh. So I asked them if we could have dinner together. We agreed to meet at my mom's on the weekend.

~

It was the Thursday morning before our weekend dinner with my parents. I was getting ready for work. He had no plans to go on the road. I overheard him giving someone directions to the apartment. I asked who was coming by. He said it was his mother.

I was on my way home from work when I saw a familiar face coming up the street. She was the sister of one of the girls he used to date before he and I got together. They happened to live nearby. I became very uneasy, largely because he had told me some time before that both sisters liked him.

When I got in I mentioned that I had seen her. He said she stopped by to say hello. He also quickly said that she stayed at the gate the whole time. I told him I was uncomfortable with it and didn't want her back at the apartment. We argued. He left and didn't come back until really late that night.

The following morning he got ready to go on the road. He didn't even have money to buy cigarettes or take the bus, yet he wanted money to go fishing with his friends. That didn't make sense to me. We were barely just getting back on our feet and didn't have that kind of money to spare. We had agreed to tighten the reigns until we got our finances in order. Why then would he be asking about money to go fishing?

We argued. He started using curse words again and slammed his hand into the door. I was so mad. He continued shouting and later made it slip that the girl he had the affair with was going to be on the so-called fishing trip. Why would he think I'd be comfortable with him being friends with her after everything that had happened? I told him to choose. It was either me or her. He made me know that they would remain friends whether I liked it or not. So I told him to leave.

The landlady called asking if everything was OK. I told her yes, apologized and promised we would keep the noise down. As soon as I came off the phone he started cursing again. I told him to leave. He packed his things but couldn't find the house keys when he was ready to go. Neither of us knew where it was. He must have thought that I hid it because he threw my handbag to the ground and started rummaging through it. I had reached my boiling point and screamed at him again to leave. I demanded he give me my bag back. He turned around, pushed me on to the bed and started choking me. I fought back and he hit me in the face. When he realized that there was a black and blue mark on my face he got up.

I told him to leave. He begged me to let him stay. He apologized and pleaded with me to give him another chance. He wanted to help me nurse my wounds. I wanted him to leave, but something made me give in instead of insisting he go.

For the next few days he made every effort to attend to my every whim. Truth is, there was nothing much for him to do because I wouldn't allow him to touch me. I didn't want him in my space. I said nothing to him for days. I was so mad. I was mad because he choked me, mad because he hit me, mad because I was forced to lie to my parents to explain the black and blue mark on my face. I was mad because I was forced to lie to my colleagues at work to hide the shame I felt.

I ignored him. It was like he wasn't there. So all he did for weeks was smoked, drank rum, and watched porn. One day he blew up at me. He said it was my fault he choked me and hit me in the face. He made me know that he was angry because I had done nothing for him, nothing for the relationship. He had expected that by now I would have used my connections to get him a job, take a loan to help him open his own company, or at least keep the car so he could use it to do business.

I listened and all I could think was to have my friends beat him up. I came to my senses pretty quickly and decided instead to move out and not let him know where I'd gone. As far as I was concerned, if he had no intention of taking responsibility for attacking me he was likely to do it again.

CHAPTER 8

I started my new job and the third week in they sent me on training. On my first day of training I walked in and already seated was a Nigerian who immediately introduced himself. He asked if I was a Christian. I hesitated a bit then said no. He asked if I would be interested in becoming one. I said yes and he proceeded to pray with me. That wasn't my first time praying the prayer of Salvation but I had hoped it would be my last.

~

I was back from training and met a young lady who told me that they had Bible Study meetings each Friday evening at the office. She extended an invitation.

The first meeting was exciting. We spent time praying, reading the Bible and sharing. I felt so at home that I decided to go back the following Friday.

~

I began my search for a new apartment but found nothing. It reminded me of how hard it was to find where we lived now. I asked a colleague from school if he knew of anywhere. He didn't but we struck up a conversation that lasted for hours. It was so much fun that we fast became friends and made plans to be study partners.

Andrew and I chatted every day. We saw each other more and more and even hung out at his house a few times.

One day he dropped me home. We sat in the car chatting for hours. We talked about things we both liked such as music, travel, and food. It was great.

After Andrew drove off I went inside. The place was dark like no-one was home. I was anxious, hoping that he had moved out. No such luck. He was still there. He was in the dark. He was crying. He was hurt because he saw me talking to Andrew for hours while I hadn't spoken to him like that for weeks. I actually felt my heart skip a beat, like old feelings that seemed long gone were coming back to life. We talked for a while. It felt good.

Day by day we fell back into our routine. This time however we talked more. We even started having dinner together every evening. We both were making a concerted effort to salvage our relationship.

Andrew and I still chatted but I was careful not to get too close. One day he dropped me home. This time we didn't stay in the car and chat. Andrew drove off and I went inside. There he was crying again. It was obvious to him that Andrew had feelings for me and I entertained them. Funny how some men think it's OK for them to flirt and cheat but the moment there is a hint of you being interested in another man or vice versa they behave as though the world has ended. I didn't take it on. I wasn't going down that road. I didn't want to argue.

~

My visits to the Bible study group became more consistent. I found myself sharing about my relationship, the loss of my child and life in general. It felt like what I expected therapy to feel like. I felt like weights had been lifted from my shoulders.

As I talked about my relationship I realized how much the last year had carried me down a path that was so unhealthy that I had lost myself. It made me wonder if starting over with him really made any sense at all. It was almost like it didn't matter that things were looking up. I felt like I just needed to make a clean break in order to find myself again.

~

I came home from work one evening and he was gone. I didn't expect it. He hadn't said he'd be going out. When he came home he went straight to the bathroom and had a shower but said nothing about where he was. Nor did he apologize for leaving without saying that he would be gone. So I asked him about it. He started complaining that I was trying to control him. I wondered if he was on drugs because of how erratic he became. I then reminded him that we had agreed to tell each other where we'd be for safety reasons. He told me it was no big deal. Then said he was moving out because he needed space.

Weeks passed and we barely spoke but I was OK. I loved being on my own. Going consistently to Bible study, praying more and having people around my age to share with also made me feel stronger.

~

He called to borrow money as his parents were having serious financial difficulties. I said sure since I knew how hard it could get sometimes. He picked me up from my office. We headed to the bank and then to buy gas for his parents' car. We talked about getting back together and about him moving back in. We made no concrete decisions but decided we would talk some more, later that evening.

He dropped me back at my office which is even closer now to where he used to work. Instead of going upstairs I walked over to the hip strip to buy lunch. I saw his parents' vehicle which was strange since he said he was heading back home which was in the opposite direction. I walked over to the parking lot to see what he was up to because in the pit of my stomach I knew he had gone to meet up with the girl he had had the affair with. There he was. He was placing the envelope with money I just gave him into her hands.

I bought lunch, walked back to my office and ate. I messaged Andrew and told him to pick me up after work. He dropped me home but this time he came inside. All I could think was that being with someone else would make me feel better.

After Andrew left I went on my laptop to check emails. I opened Gmail and started combing through when I suddenly realized that I was in his inbox and not mine. There were emails from the girl he had been having the affair with, the girl that lived nearby, her sister, and some other women. There was even one from the ex that he lived with when we met. In some of his emails he said nasty things about me. He also admitted that he was only with me because he felt it was a way to get out of his financial rut.

In another email he was flirting with his ex's sister, the one who had 'stayed at the gate the whole time'. They had made plans for her to come over and make out in my apartment on my bed. It was just too much.

I was about to close the laptop when I saw another email. In it he was making plans to go to Canada, he and his wife. I reread the email. He had referred to the girl he had the affair with as his wife. I shut down the laptop and went to bed.

The following day I went to work and cried on the shoulders of the leader of our Bible study group. I cried because I had wasted a year and a half with this man. I cried because I had decided to sleep with Andrew in an attempt to somehow heal my broken heart. Yet all it did was deepen the wounds I had been carrying, perhaps from as far back as my childhood. I cried because I was now worried that my ex may have given me a sexually transmitted disease or worse, HIV. I cried because I had allowed myself to sink into an emotional, financial, and mental mess. *(Fact: So many women get into relationships and because of their mushy emotions, allow themselves to make unwise calls about how they handle sex. Invariably many women end up having unprotected sex. Unprotected sex may result in STDs and unwanted pregnancy. My stance is abstinence. However if you choose to have sex, please use a condom.)*

At the end of my tears my Bible study leader reminded me that God would keep me: *"He shields all who take refuge in Him"* [2 Samuel 22:31].

~

He called the next day. I told him there was no way we would get back together.

CHAPTER 9

The break up pushed me closer to God. I grew closer to Him daily. I stopped cursing, partying, and hardly drank alcohol. I found myself praying more, reading my Bible more, and listening to gospel music more. I also spent more time talking to God throughout the day. Even then, I still had a long way to go. Three months after the break up and I was now seeing Andrew, Mike and Dane.

The problem with Andrew was that he was very preoccupied with work. Most of his time was spent there. He wanted me to move in with him and talked about marriage but I had little feelings for him because we hardly spent time together.

Mike on the other hand was someone I had liked many years before but he had moved overseas. We met again at a music festival and from then on spent quite a bit of time hanging out.

Dane worked in my office. He kept sending me cute messages. At first I wasn't interested but then he and his fiancée broke off their engagement which suddenly made him seem quite appealing.

I was dating all three men. If you can call it that! *(Fact: Emotional wounds require immediate attention. Healing can only come with prayer and spiritual counselling. If not dealt with, wounds deepen leading you along a downward spiral, as was the case with me. Though I was growing as a Christian I still felt I needed companionship in order to feel good about myself.)*

~

I wanted nothing to do with my ex. For more than a year I avoided his calls and ignored his emails. Then I moved. Andrew told me about a place that was closer to work. It was a fully furnished super studio which was cheaper, larger, and cozier than the apartment I lived in with my ex.

~

One day my ex happened to come by my mom's and I was there. I went outside to speak with him. He wanted to apologize for everything. He wanted me to see that he had changed, had grown up and was now a responsible man. I didn't care. He told me about the business that he had started with a friend of his. It was doing well. They even had a company car. I didn't care. He thanked me for allowing him to apologize and asked for my forgiveness. I had forgiven him. I just didn't care.

We saw each other again when one of his friends attempted suicide. He called because according to him I was the only person he could talk to about it. I took his call. He asked to come over and oddly enough I gave him my new address. We chatted. I prayed with him. He left.

~

It was over a year before my ex and I spoke again. By then I had started going to a local church where I got baptized and joined their choir and prayer team. I even had a Bible study going at my apartment. Of course I stopped seeing Andrew, Mike and Dane.

At first I thought it was strange. My ex had called to ask about God. He had been reading one of my dad's books, 'Christ Died for Me, Christ Lives in Me'. It had left him with many questions about God. In fact, he had asked God to enter his life. He was now a Christian.

We spoke a few times after that and I explained how much I was in love with God, how He had changed my life and how serving Him was the best thing to ever happen to me. My ex said he wanted the same thing. He said he wanted to be baptized and wanted me to help him on this journey in whatever way I could. I was now convinced that he had turned his life around.

This was the start of a new relationship. Deep down I felt this time it would work.

~

It was my wedding day. Everything was perfect. My dad agreed to officiate. My dad paid for everything. He called his friends at the Bridal Place and they arranged the whole thing in three days. The colors were exactly what I wanted. The food was delicious. The service was fantastic. The lawns were immaculate and plush. The room where we had the ceremony was beautiful. To top it all off I had the perfect dress, a Mercedes original.

The road to get here was rocky but we were different people now. We did premarital counselling and that helped to put things into perspective. We even had a plan this time around. I left my job but had several opportunities lined up. He was also having discussions with a large real estate firm. They wanted him to come on board as property manager. We had what appeared to be a solid foundation on which to start our new life.

~

Clearly I was meant to be the poster girl for one of these soap opera dramas because I went from "I do" to "I don't" in six months. This is what happened:

Starting a new job took longer than expected. The company had several issues to straighten out prior to me filling the position. His job also fell through. They hired internally instead. In the middle of all that I fell ill, though neither of us realized it at first. I thought it was insomnia brought on by the stress of not working. Then I realized I was losing weight. I lost 50 pounds in 2 months. I was really weak. That left him to take care of all the household chores. He resented that. He spent half his time complaining to anyone who would listen that I was lazy and didn't know how to be a wife.

Like so many times before I didn't realize that he was upset. He was so upset that one day he swore at me and again threatened to kill me. He told me I was lucky to have married him because nobody else wanted me. He told me that I was the worst kind of wife a man could have. He implied that I had little worth to him and so he was forced to cheat. I said nothing but just stayed near the knife rack just in case he tried to attack me. He ranted for close to an hour then walked out. He disappeared for days.

The first night he walked out I stared at the ceiling for hours. I was amazed that we had come full circle. That nothing had changed. What was I thinking? I had escaped. I was free. How did I get pulled back in? Then all the memories from two years before came flooding back. It was like I was reliving the fright of our relationship all over again. I got up and bolted the door.

How could I have forgotten those nights back then when I didn't want to fall asleep because I was afraid he'd try to kill me? Or the shame I felt because of the lies he told people about me? The tantrums he threw and the name calling whenever he didn't get his way? The physical abuse? The emotional and verbal abuse? The trauma? How could I have been so foolish? How could I have married this man? To come back and have to deal with the same things all over again.

~

My marriage was filled with anguish, fear and distress. I guess I only had myself to blame. I had rushed back into this relationship believing that everything would be great because we were both Christians now. Yet, truth is, some Christians make no attempt to change their bad ways. Furthermore changing takes time.

The Bible speaks of using wisdom, but where was the wisdom in getting back together with him, and so quickly at that? Where was the wisdom in rushing to get married to someone who needed help? Where was the wisdom in getting married when I needed help myself? Then I thought "OK, you're in it but why stay so long?" It was because I had convinced myself that this was how it was with newlyweds as they tried to get to know each other. That too was a lie.

This needed to stop. I wanted it to be over but I was afraid. I was afraid that walking away would displease God. I had always heard that divorce was wrong. On the other hand, I couldn't fathom why God would want me to stay with this man. Then it hit me. God loves marriage and so like everything else He would want me to give it my best and I wasn't really sure that I had.

~

We had been going to a different church for some time after getting married and so decided to go see one of the pastors there. It was our only hope. We were separated and living apart. He hadn't been back since he stormed out weeks before.

The pastor prayed with us, laid down the ground rules then opened the floor for us to share our feelings.

My husband went first. I listened intently. Everything he said about me and about our marriage highlighted the fact that we should never have been married in the first place. His perspectives on my role as wife were absurd. He believed that submission meant subservience. He expected me to ask how high when he said jump, give up on my dreams so his could be realized, and agree with every opinion he had, even if it made me uncomfortable. In his mind his needs superseded mine. Therefore any objection from me would give him the right to debase and abuse me.

It was my turn to speak. However, every time I opened my mouth he cut me off. He disagreed with everything I said. He had an excuse for everything. I decided it was pointless. I said very little thereafter.

I said very little as I headed home. I wanted to scream but couldn't and though I knew it was time to end my marriage I couldn't help but ask myself, How will it look? What will people say? How do I explain being married for less than the time it took to plan my wedding?

CHAPTER 10

I felt trapped. I couldn't believe that this is what it all had come to. I prayed. I bawled. I screamed. I argued with God. Then I sat down, and opened my diary. I began writing.

Dear Diary,

Where's the girl who knew growing up that you had to love yourself first before you can truly love someone else? If I really understood what to expect of love I wouldn't have married this man with his controlling and aggressive spirit. I wouldn't be contemplating now whether to stay or go.

I spent years writing down what I wanted from marriage and love but I'm realizing now that I have no clue what love should look like.

1 Corinthians 13:4-7 says *"Love is patient, love is kind. It does not envy, it does not boast, it is not proud. It does not dishonor others, it is not self-seeking, it is not easily angered, it keeps no record of wrongs. Love does not delight in evil but rejoices with the truth. It always protects, always trusts, always hopes, always perseveres"*. I had to admit I wasn't sure what all that meant.

I closed my diary and started thinking about what 1 Corinthians 13 said about love. After much prayer and some research it started to all make sense. I wrote down my thoughts.

Dear Diary,

This is what love[3] should look like:

1) **Love is patient.** Patience involves us quickly forgiving and forgetting when we make each other angry or annoy each other. It's spending more time listening and less time talking. It's taking the time to reason things out together. It's agreeing to disagree when you both can't seem to agree.

2) **Love is kind.** Kindness is saying kind words that compliment, empower and encourage. It's making every effort to make the other person feel good about him or herself. It's about being thoughtful, tender and having a big heart towards each other. It's showing concern when the other person is hurting, sad or exhibiting some other kind of negative disposition. It's about giving to each other by virtue of our time, possessions, blessings, gifts and everything else that's good.

3) **Love does not envy.** To not envy means not being jealous of possessions, blessings, gifts or achievements, but instead rejoicing when the other person rejoices. It's about wanting great things for each other. It also means not having an inflated sense of entitlement or trying to compete with the other person to show yourself more valuable than

---

[3] Useful articles on the characteristics of Love can be accessed at www.gotquestions.org.

you are. In the sight of God we are all valuable: *"For God does not show favoritism"* [Romans 2:11].

4) **Love does not boast.** To not boast means not bragging in order to make yourself feel and look good. It's not seeking to be the center of attention at the other person's expense. It's about not dominating the conversation in order to exaggerate one's importance.

5) **Love is not proud.** Since love is not proud we shouldn't expect to always be right. We should recognize that we have weaknesses and should know that we can be wrong. We should be willing to say I'm sorry or to compromise, even when we're right. Not being proud is being open to the idea of asking for help rather than insisting that things be done your way.

6) **Love does not dishonor others.** To not dishonor means to not disrespect. It means not swearing at each other, calling each other derogatory names, or saying things to intentionally hurt each other. It's about not throwing things at each other or showing other signs of aggression. It means we don't put each other down, flirt with other men or women, criticize each other, complain about each other or raise our voices in front of others. It means we shouldn't repeatedly disappoint each other. It also means we should appreciate that no means no.

7) **Love is not self-seeking.** To not be self-seeking means to not be selfish. Rather, it's seeking to make each other happy. It's caring for the other person more than you do yourself. It means focusing on each other's needs and concerns and how one's actions will affect the other person. It means not using emotional blackmail or selfish demands to get one's own way. It means loving without condition instead of choosing to be together because of what you expect to gain from the relationship.

8) **Love is not easily angered.** Not being easily angered means not being easily provoked or offended. It means having self-control rather than being quick to become annoyed or get into a temper. It's about not being touchy, intimidating or confrontational.

9) **Love keeps no record of wrongs.** To not keep record of wrongs means to not keep a log of each other's mistakes. It means we shouldn't hold the mistakes or sins from the past against each other or repeatedly bring them up. Instead, we should look beyond all that, expecting greater things.

10) **Love does not delight in evil but rejoices with the truth.** To not delight in evil means that we shouldn't gloat over each other's guilt. That means we shouldn't rejoice when the other person makes a mistake or is caught in sin or misfortune. It also means, however, that when one person is wrong the other needs to gently say so and help that

person do better. Rejoicing with the truth means we should celebrate good behaviors and virtues.

11) **Love always protects.** Since love always protects, we should make the other person feel safe at all times on all levels - physical, emotional, spiritual, mental, and financial. We should always keep each other safe. That also requires that we stick by each other in situations of emotional, mental, physical and/or financial distress.

12) **Love always trusts.** "Love always trusts" means not being suspicious of the person that you claim to love. It's about not believing the worst or being skeptical about the other person. It therefore means giving each other the benefit of the doubt in every situation.

13) **Love always hopes.** "Love always hopes" means never seeing failure or mistakes as final. It means seeing the potential in the other person and believing the best about them. It's having hope in your future together which is dependent on the trust you share.

14) **Love always perseveres.** Since love always perseveres it means it is unyielding. It keeps going and going. It means not giving up on each other. It's telling each other that you'll make it regardless of the situation. It's the two of you believing that you will make it.

As I read and reread my notes I came to the realization that I wasn't in a loving relationship. I burst into tears. I cried for hours. Then the crying stopped. It was like someone turned off the tap. I felt so at peace. I almost forgot why I was crying in the first place.

I no longer felt that I would be condemned to hell if I left my husband. Instead, I felt like no matter my decision, God would pull me through. The Bible says *"In all things God works for the good of those who love Him, who have been called according to His purpose"* [Rom 8:28]. I love God. He's the most important person in my life. I've been called according to His purpose. So everything will be great.

I went to bed. The next day I told my husband I wanted a divorce.

PART 2
THE KEYS TO MY HEALING

This section of the book was written to help you heal from wounds you may be carrying from your relationship(s), current or past. It explains the keys I used to heal. I hope it brings you healing, too.

Through the Eyes of Love
by Ripton P Morris

I see new beauty in my surrounds
Life springing from the dewy grounds
Bears dancing with the swaying trees
Eagles soaring on a gentle breeze
I raise a praise to my GOD above
I'm seeing through the eyes of Love

God's love has purified my view
My taste buds have become as new
Romantic songs play o'er the din
Unfettered passions burn within
I smell fresh flowers in a sunlit cove
I'm looking through the eyes of Love

Step 1
Determine If It's a Bad Relationship

In this step I've included two questionnaires that will help
you evaluate the actions, behaviors or habits that your
spouse/other half may display, as well as some of your own
feelings. The purpose is not to condemn him, but to help
you reflect on and assess the quality of your relationship.
Please give careful thought as you choose your responses.

Survey I: He Loves Me, He Loves Me Not

Answer all questions by circling 1 for True or 0 for False. Answer true if he does this most of the time.

True or false; he's patient with you. He....	True	False
1. Quickly forgives and forgets when you make him angry or you annoy him	1	0
2. Spends more time listening and less time talking when you need him to be there for you	1	0
3. Reasons things out with you	1	0
4. Doesn't try to make you feel that you're not smart enough	1	0
5. Agrees to disagree when you don't see eye to eye	1	0

True or false; he's kind to you. He....	True	False
6. Says kind words that compliment you, empower you, encourage you, and make you feel good about yourself	1	0
7. Is thoughtful, tender, and has a big heart towards you	1	0
8. Shows concern when you're hurting, sad, or showing some other negative disposition	1	0
9. Shares his time, possessions, blessings, and gifts with you	1	0

True or false; he isn't envious of you. He....	**True**	**False**
10. Isn't jealous of your possessions, blessings, gifts, or achievements	1	0
11. Rejoices when you rejoice and wants great things for you	1	0
12. Doesn't have an inflated sense of entitlement	1	0
13. Doesn't try to compete with you to show that he is more valuable than you are	1	0

True or false; he isn't boastful. He....	**True**	**False**
14. Doesn't brag in order to make himself feel and look good	1	0
15. Doesn't seek to be the center of attention at your expense	1	0
16. Doesn't dominate the conversation in order to exaggerate his importance	1	0

True or false; he isn't proud. He....	**True**	**False**
17. Doesn't always expect to be right	1	0
18. Recognizes that he has weaknesses and knows that he can be wrong too	1	0
19. Is willing to say he's sorry	1	0
20. Compromises even if he's right	1	0
21. Is open to the idea of asking for help	1	0

	True	False
22. Doesn't always insist that things be done his way	1	0

True or false; he doesn't dishonor you. He....

	True	False
23. Doesn't disrespect you	1	0
24. Doesn't swear at you, call you derogatory names, or say things to intentionally hurt you	1	0
25. Doesn't' slam the door in your face, throw things at you, or show signs of aggression towards you	1	0
26. Doesn't put you down, flirt with other women, criticize you, complain about you, or raise his voice at you in front of others	1	0
27. Doesn't repeatedly let you down or string you along	1	0
28. Appreciates that no means no	1	0

True or false; he isn't self-seeking. He....

	True	False
29. Isn't selfish	1	0
30. Doesn't care for himself more than he does you	1	0
31. Seeks to make you happy	1	0
32. Doesn't want to be with you just because of what you can do for him	1	0

	True	False
33. Focuses on your needs and concerns and cares how his actions affect you	1	0
34. Doesn't use emotional blackmail or selfish demands to get his own way	1	0

True or false; he isn't easily angered. He....	True	False
35. Isn't easily provoked or offended	1	0
36. Isn't quick to become annoyed or get into a temper	1	0
37. Isn't touchy, intimidating, or confrontational	1	0

True or false; he doesn't keep records of wrongs. He....	True	False
38. Doesn't keep a log of your mistakes	1	0
39. Doesn't hold the mistakes or sins from your past against you	1	0
40. Doesn't repeatedly bring up your mistakes or sins	1	0
41. Looks beyond your past mistakes and flaws expecting greater things	1	0

True or false; he doesn't delight in evil but rejoices in the truth. He….	True	False
42. Doesn't gloat over your guilt	1	0
43. Doesn't rejoice when you are caught in sin or misfortune	1	0
44. Gently says when you're wrong	1	0
45. Helps you to do better	1	0
46. Celebrates you	1	0
47. Celebrates your good behavior and virtues	1	0

True or false; he protects you. He….	True	False
48. Always makes you feel safe	1	0
49. Always keeps you safe	1	0
50. Sticks by your side, even in situations that bring emotional, mental, physical, or financial distress	1	0

True or false; he trusts you. He….	True	False
51. Isn't suspicious of you	1	0
52. Gives you the benefit of the doubt	1	0
53. Doesn't believe the worst about you	1	0

True or false; he is hopeful. He….	True	False
54. Sees potential in you	1	0
55. Believes the best about you	1	0
56. Is hopeful about your future	1	0

True or false; he is one who perseveres. He….	True	False
57. Never gives up on you	1	0
58. Tells you you'll make it in every situation	1	0
59. Believes that the two of you will make it	1	0

After completing the survey add up your total score. Scores between 52 and 59 suggest you're in a very good relationship. Scores between 47 and 51 suggest you're in a good relationship. Scores between 41 and 46 suggest you two need help and could perhaps improve your relationship with counselling. Scores below 41 suggest you may need to exit the relationship.

If you scored 46 or below I encourage you to complete Survey II.

Survey II: Am I in An Abusive Relationship?

Answer True or False. Answer true if this happens sometimes.

Sometimes HE...	True	False
1. Expects you to do things his way even if that makes you feel uncomfortable	☐	☐
2. Says or does things that cause your children/family/friends or others to turn against you	☐	☐
3. Criticizes, humiliates, or degrades you	☐	☐
4. Blames you for everything that goes wrong even if it's his fault	☐	☐
5. Finds fault with everything you say or do	☐	☐
6. Curses at you or calls you derogatory names	☐	☐
7. Makes fun of, brushes you off, or ignores you when you try to talk to him	☐	☐
8. Stomps his feet, hits you, punches you, or stares at you in an uncomfortable way	☐	☐
9. Clenches his fist, jaws, or teeth when he gets annoyed, angry, or frustrated with you	☐	☐
10. Kicks, bangs, or throws things when he gets annoyed, angry, or frustrated with you	☐	☐
11. Uses physical force or threatens you to get his own way	☐	☐

	True	False
12. Threatens to harm you or your loved ones	☐	☐
13. Threatens to kill you or your loved ones	☐	☐
14. Speaks loudly, yells or spits at you	☐	☐
15. Steals from you	☐	☐
16. Flirts with other women in front of you and/or people you know	☐	☐
17. Stops you from spending time with close friends or family members	☐	☐

Sometimes YOU…	True	False
18. Feel nervous or afraid whenever he's around	☐	☐
19. Worry that you'll say or do the wrong things because it will make him angry or annoyed	☐	☐
20. Rush home from wherever you are for fear that he'll become angry or annoyed	☐	☐
21. Skip work and/or school because of bodily marks, scars, or bruises he gave you	☐	☐
22. Skip work and/or school because he threatened you, criticized you, or made you feel badly about yourself	☐	☐
23. Cry for hours because of the stress, sadness, or fear you're feeling from being in the relationship with him	☐	☐

	True	False
24. Fear for your life or the life of your children, loved ones, or friends	☐	☐
25. Wish you would die because of how he makes you feel	☐	☐
26. Think of killing yourself because of how he makes you feel	☐	☐

If you've selected 'True' in response to any of the questions above you are in an abusive relationship. It suggests that you have been verbally, emotionally and/or physically abused.

A 'True' response suggests that you should seek professional help. Call or visit a women's shelter, domestic violence hotline or center, abuse helpline, pastor or the police. Don't be afraid to take back your life.

This questionnaire was developed based on my own experience. However, similar questionnaires can be found online. I found these online tools to be very useful as I pulled together my own questionnaires. Online sources are:
- http://www.endthefear.co.uk/questionnaire/
- http://www.hiddenhurt.co.uk/questionnaire.html
- http://psychcentral.com/quizzes/dvquiz.htm
- http://www.helpguide.org/articles/abuse/domestic-violence-and-abuse.htm
- http://liveboldandbloom.com/11/relationships/signs -of-emotional-abuse

Step 2
Take Steps To Heal

He is I AM
by Ripton P Morris

He is I AM
Ever present in the present

He is I AM
Never past, always here, always now

He is I AM
He isn't was; He is

He is I AM
He isn't will be; He is

He is I AM
And I am His

THE HEALING PROCESS

My healing process unfolded step by step as follows:
1. Ending my relationship with my husband
2. Filling the void created by our separation
3. Receiving the Gift of Salvation who is Jesus Christ
4. Repenting of things I did wrong in the relationship
5. Claiming my healing
6. Speaking affirmations over my life

Ending my relationship

I ended my relationship with my husband. I made a clean break. I told him in a matter of fact, face to face conversation that it was over and made it clear that I would not be moving forward with our marriage. This was important because I had to be sure that he took me seriously and knew not to make any effort to change my mind.

Because of the threatening nature of our relationship I ensured that the break up was done out in the open and in a safe place. He came by my mother's home and I told him at the gate. I felt comfortable, but knew that if this tactic didn't work I'd have to get help. My back up plan was to call the police and have them escort me to his parent's house. In addition, I was prepared to take out a restraining order against him. *(Although I didn't need to get the police involved, you may be one of those who should. Evaluate the nature of your relationship with your spouse/other half and if you feel he may want to harm you because you've decided to walk away, call the police. Don't wait until it's too late before soliciting their help. You see, the problem quite often is that we try to fix things on our own. That was certainly my mistake. What we need to do instead is ask for help. Remember we sometimes get so caught up in our emotions that we can't think straight, which means we need help if we're to make wise decisions. We would also need help if our spouse/other half is physically stronger and thus able to overpower us. We ought to tell our family members, close friends and/or trusted church leaders what we're going through the moment we feel undue stress or see any abusive patterns emerging. They usually mean us well and will give us the spiritual, emotional and/or physical support we need.)*

Break ups require that we not only say it's over but demonstrate it. As such, after my conversation with my husband I:

- Threw away everything that tied me to him including my wedding rings, the clothes his mom had given me, etcetera.

- Deleted all conversations we had via email, SMS, WhatsApp or other social media.

- Ended all communication with him. I've only chatted with him twice in recent weeks – 8 months after I ended the relationship. This was only after I decided that I was sufficiently healed. Furthermore, we chatted by WhatsApp, not face to face or by telephone.

- Limited my conversations about him. After the break up I hardly spoke about him. The only conversations I had were those with pastors or leaders of my church who played a role in helping me heal my wounds, and to some extent, my parents who are my confidants.

For me, the clean break from him was particularly important, as anything else would have resulted in us going back and forth. No healing can take place under those conditions. It was also important for me to speak to him face to face when telling him it was over, because anything else would be taken lightly by him. *(A clean break may not be possible for everyone. Some of you may find that you can't just delete him from your life right away as you may need information from conversations, letters etcetera to help you in settling your divorce or separation. On the other hand, if you're like me and can afford to make that clean break, I encourage you to do so and bring closure to your life. Making that clean break may even require for safety reasons that you end the relationship by telephone or mail rather than face to face. Others may even think it best not to say anything at all but just disappear. If he is dangerous don't hesitate to walk away without saying anything. Whatever the case is, be honest with yourself and make wise decisions.)*

Filling the void created by the separation

Figuring out what to do with myself in order to break out of the routine we had formed was a little tricky. I needed to create my own routines. Essentially, I needed to form new habits and ways of doing things; things that empowered me, brought me joy and kept me focused on a positive future without him.

As such, every night before bed I planned what I'd do the next day. This was critical to my healing process. Here's why. Waiting until the next day to decide what to do would leave me feeling sad, listless and discombobulated. Whenever that happened I'd succumb to these moments of weakness and find myself fantasizing about getting back together with him.

So to avoid that, I thought through my routine for the following day from the night before and then once the day started I stuck by that predetermined schedule.

My drive to fill the void left behind by the separation from my husband also led me to recommit my life to God. This for me was even more fulfilling than anything else I had ever done. It then informed the kind of activities I engaged in. For example, I became more involved at church and later went to Bible School. That gave me so much energy and joy that I went on to do voluntary work. *(Some of you may think this is not for you but honestly, I found that being involved at church helped to ground me spiritually and emotionally, and ultimately that's what I needed, particularly after going through such a dreadful ordeal. Volunteering, spending time with family and friends or even alone were also great ways to fill the void.)*

Receiving the Gift of Salvation, who is Jesus Christ

I had been saved and baptized prior to marrying my husband. However, I felt that the trauma of the relationship, including how I responded to him sometimes, in ways that were unchristian and not becoming of a godly wife, had somehow strained my relationship with God, specifically my prayer and worship life. For this reason I decided to recommit my life to God.

It's not that I felt like I had lost the Gift of Salvation I had been given when I first received Jesus Christ as my Savior. On the contrary, I merely felt that making the commitment again would signal to God that my heart towards Him was one of total surrender. As a preacher once taught, *'Make God your husband. Spend time dating him. Get into an intimate relationship with Him. He'll then teach you how to be a good wife and once He's made you the best wife you can be, He'll honor you by giving you the best husband there is for you'.*

I encourage all of you reading this to receive Jesus Christ as Lord and Savior. If you've done so already that's fantastic. You've already made the best decision you'll ever make in your lifetime. If you did so long ago but believe that the stress, disappointment or trauma you've been through has separated you from God in anyway, then make a new commitment.

Receiving the Gift of Salvation is simple. As Ripton P Morris (2010) writes: *"Salvation is a gift that is made available to those who repent, believe and confess that Jesus is Lord and that He died and rose from the dead to save all mankind. This Gift cannot be earned from good deeds or by simply being 'good'. It is a matter of faith, acting on what you believe according to God's Word. If you desire a change in your life, and if you are seeking the peace that is found only through a personal relationship with Jesus Christ, then you are at the right place. He is ready and willing to help you right now, right where you are."*

If you are ready to receive the Gift of Salvation, who is Jesus Christ, or ready to recommit to Him, repeat the following prayer aloud. Bear in mind reading it aloud will give life to your words in the same way God's words were given life when He spoke the earth into being:

"Dear Jesus, Your Word says, 'Whosoever shall call on the name of the Lord shall be saved.' I call on You, Jesus, to come into my heart and be Lord of my life. I confess that You are Lord, and I believe in my heart that God raised you from the dead. Thank You, for saving me; break

91

me and mold me into what You want me to be; and use me for Your glory. Amen." (Morris, 2010).

It is recommended that you then find a Bible teaching church and let them know your decision. Be sure to find out if they have a discipleship, nurture or new beginners' class. These classes are very helpful in teaching you more on how to maintain your relationship with God through Scripture, prayer and praise.

The Gift
by Ripton P Morris

Everyone falls short of His glory
But that's not the end of the story
GOD gave us the Gift of Salvation
For everyone from every nation

Not a thing to buy, no works to do
His grace extended to me and you
Jesus the Lamb for our sins crucified
Raised up again, now we're justified

He's a Gift only if you're a receiver
Turn your back on that old deceiver
Bend your knee; lift your heart and say

Dear Jesus, I believe in my heart today
You died for my sins and God raised You
Your blood saved me and I praise You
Send Your Spirit to comfort, to guide
And to teach me how to abide – Amen

Repenting of things I did wrong in the relationship

Repentance is critical to healing. It involves taking responsibility for wrongs, known and unknown, then asking God for forgiveness. At first I was convinced that my husband was entirely to blame for our failed marriage. As I talked to God and asked Him to reveal to me where I went wrong He showed me otherwise. He explained that though my husband was wrong to have done the things he did, I was also wrong.

Fact is, I wasn't a submissive wife. Notice I say submissive and not subservient. God expects the husband to love and submit to his wife [1 Peter 3:7]. He also expects that the wife will submit to her husband by showing him respect and regarding him as head of the family. I didn't do a good job of that.

The Lord showed me that I was haughty, feisty, retaliatory, and the list went on. He showed me that in my attempt to defend myself mentally and emotionally from my husband, I dishonored him, which dishonors God. He also showed me that I was disrespectful when I cursed back at my husband, made plans to have my friends beat him up, and prayed that he not come back every time he left the house.

Those examples made sense. However, what didn't make sense to me was when the Lord said I tried too much to be the man of the house. For example those times when my husband couldn't find money to pay the bills and rather than let him sort it out I went and paid them. Naturally, I thought I was helping but really what I did was usurped his role as provider.

The Lord also told me that I erred by:

- Not spending enough time praying for my husband.
- Not fighting enough for my marriage using prayer, praise, worship and affirmations.
- Not preparing for marriage as I convinced myself that all I needed to do was to be a good cook and home keeper. However, marriage requires much more.
- Trying to do things in my own strength instead of allowing Him (God) to fix them.
- Trying to win my husband over with words, rather than with my behavior [1 Peter 3:1-2].

The revelation was shocking for me and caused me to change the way I was praying. I prayed aloud asking God to forgive me for each of my sins as I called them out one by one. I also forgave myself. I then asked Him to help me become the woman, wife, mother, friend, sibling, daughter, co-worker, neighbor, employee, boss and everything else He called me to be. I just didn't think it made sense that I would be a great friend or neighbor but not be a great mother. Or that I would be a great mother yet not a great neighbor - we're either living right or we're not. I needed God to transform my thinking, actions and reactions.

I thought my prayers were over, but then the Lord showed me that I hadn't prayed for my husband. So I prayed aloud. I forgave him for each of the things he did. I called them out one by one. I also asked God to forgive him and bless him [Luke 6:28]. I prayed that he would be transformed, that he would be made a better man, husband, father, son, friend, co-worker, neighbor, employee, boss and everything else God called him to be. I prayed for his soul; that he would truly come to know God. I ended by forgiving his parents, relatives and friends who had hurt me. I blessed them and asked God to transform them as well.

Claiming my healing

My ultimate aim was to be healed. I realized I needed to claim that healing through prayer. I started by renouncing the negative words spoken over me by my husband, his parents and others related to him. I also needed to renounce any negative words I had spoken over myself. For instance, those times when I said 'I guess I was never meant to be married' or when I said 'I'd rather be alone than be unhappy.' Bottom line is, every negative word, every curse word, every derogatory word, and every death word had to be broken from over my life.

I repeated the following prayer over several days:

"Dear Lord, I thank you for loving me when I didn't love myself. I thank you for forgiving me even when I chose the lies of the enemy. Lies that made me believe that what was being said about me was true. Now Lord, I renounce every evil word, every curse word, every death word, every derogatory word spoken over my life by my husband, others related to him, or even by me, in Jesus' name. I renounce humiliation, rejection, fear, worthlessness, low self-esteem, shame, anger, disappointment, depression, unforgiveness, heartbreak and anything else I haven't mentioned. I now speak life, healing, blessings and prosperity over my life. I declare that I shall live and not die. I shall live to accomplish Your Will for my life, in Jesus' name. Amen."

Sometime after that a friend introduced me to Katie Souza's program, Healing Your Soul: Real keys to the Miraculous, Episode 2[4]. In that episode Souza explained, *"When Jesus shed his blood on the cross it washed away every sin that could ever wound your soul…whether you sinned against yourself or someone sinned against you or even your ancestors sinned and made a wound in their soul and then passed it down to you".*

As I listened to the program I realised that I desperately needed healing for my soul. At the end of her program she invited her viewers to pray. I found myself repeating the words aloud. I prayed:

"Dear Jesus, I ask forgiveness for any sin that I committed that wounded my soul. Wash me clean of all my sins, the sins of my ancestors and also any sins committed against me. I've put your blood on those sins, and I also forgive people who hurt me. Leviticus 17 says your blood atones for my soul, so I believe your blood is washing me clean of every sin in my soul right now. I receive your forgiveness, in Jesus' Name. Amen."

Souza then invited us to place ours hand on our stomach while saying the prayer below. I repeated aloud:

"Lord Jesus, sin has wounded my soul, but your dunamis (power) can heal every wound inside of me. I've already been resurrected to a new life in you so dunamis lives in my spirit. I decree it's flowing into my soul right now and causing me to be excellent of soul. Heal every wound inside of me. Cause my soul to be excellent in every place where I've been injured. Fill me with the resurrection power in both my soul and my body. I know when my soul gets healed I will be prospered in my

---

[4] Quoted with permission.

finances and in my health, even as my soul is prospered. So, I receive my healing now, in Jesus' name. Amen"

I repeated these prayers as often as I could over the days that followed. Simply because I knew that the wounds that were created during my relationship and even before that were created over a period of time. This didn't happen overnight. It made sense then that the whole healing process would require that I spend time undoing them.

Some of you may be wondering what *dunamis* means. *Dunamis* is a Greek word used 120 times in the New Testament. According to one article, *dunamis* loosely refers to strength, power or ability and is the root word for the English words dynamite, dynamo and dynamic. Another article refers to *dunamis* as *"... power to achieve by applying the Lord's inherent abilities...Power through God's ability"* (Helps Ministries, 2011).

Speaking affirmations over my life

I was listening to Joyce Meyer one day and she spoke about the importance of believing in our hearts that we are who God says we are. This was nothing new. I had heard it from my parents and pastor before. Yet this time I felt deep down that I needed to say these words aloud, continually, over my life and circumstances just so they would have life and become real to me. Then I heard The Lord saying, *You've renounced the negative words but you need to replace them with affirmations.*

I started by acknowledging God, repeating what the Bible says about Him and who He is to me:

I love You, Lord. Abba Father, There is none like You. You are God all by yourself. You are Alpha and Omega, the Beginning and the End. You are my Father, my Redeemer, my Friend, my Advocate, the I Am that I Am. You are my Provider, my Deliverer, my Judge, my Defender. I adore You.

I then took a few verses, personalized them and spoke them over my life. *(I do this as often as I can. Bear in mind, my pastor often reminds us that this should be done daily.)*

- *"I am a friend of God"* [Exodus 33:11]
- *"I am rooted and established in Love"* [Ephesians 3:17]
- *"I am restored"* [Job 22:23]
- *"I am renewed"* [Isaiah 40:31]
- *"My soul will prosper"* [3 John 2]
- *"My soul is healed"* [Psalm 19:7]
- *"I will prosper"* [Jeremiah 29:11]
- *"I am fearfully and wonderfully made"* [Psalm 139:14]
- *"I will bear much fruit"* [John 15:5]
- *"I am anointed of God"* [1 John 2:27]
- *"My words are anointed"* [Psalm 45:2]
- *"I am the head and not the tail"* [Deuteronomy 28:13a]
- *"I am above and not beneath"* [Deuteronomy 28:13b]
- *"I am a blessing"* [Genesis 12: 3]
- *"I am blessed and highly favored"* [Luke 1:28]
- *"I am a child of God"* [John 1:12]
- *"I am a new creature"* [2 Corinthians 5:17]
- *"I have the mind of Christ"* [1 Corinthians 2:16]

- *"I am seated in heavenly places"* [Ephesians 2:6]
- *"God loves me"* [John 16:27]
- *"I am a Proverbs 31 woman"* [Proverbs 31]
- *"I have godly wisdom"* [1 Corinthians 3:19]
- *"I am royalty"* [Isaiah 62:3]
- *"I am a chosen generation"* [1 Peter 2:9]
- *"I am alive in Christ"* [Romans 6:11]
- *"I am set free"* [Galatians 5:1]
- *"No weapons formed against me will prosper"* [Isaiah 54:17]
- *"I do not have a spirit of fear but of power, love and a sound mind"* [2 Timothy 1:7]

All Poured Out
Sung by Tricia-Anne Y. Morris
Written by Ripton P Morris

I must give Jesus the whole jar
I can't hold back a drop
He has to have all my being
From my soles to my head top

All poured out
I'm all poured out
I'm all poured out for Jesus
All poured out
I'm all poured out
I'm all poured out for my Lord

Though some may say it's a big waste
I'll pour out every bit
I know I'm saved by his marvelous grace
All my guilt he has acquit

All poured out
I'm all poured out
I'm all poured out for Jesus
All poured out
I'm all poured out
I'm all poured out for my Lord

THE RESULTS

To reiterate, healing my wounds took time. It didn't happen overnight. I worked at it daily for close to a year. I planned and was deliberate, taking specific steps to ensure I regained my emotional freedom and was healed of the pains and disappointments of the past.

The changes that took place were remarkable. They were obvious to my parents, siblings, close friends, colleagues and others around me. These changes were evidenced in every area of my life: spiritual, family, physical, work, and social.

My spiritual life

The baggage I carried from my failed marriage felt like a weight. Because of it I wasn't able to pray, praise or worship the way I was accustomed to. It was like something was stifling that side of me.

With healing came transformation. Today my love affair with the Lord is far more intimate than I could ever have fathomed as a young Christian. My spiritual appetite has caused me to be more purposeful with respect to what I listen to, watch, read, or where I go. I also praise, pray, worship and meditate differently. These days when I meditate I hear new songs and music being downloaded from God.

I go to church regularly now and even find myself watching sermons because I crave the Word so much. I most enjoy Joyce Meyer, TD Jakes and Myles Munroe. I also enjoy

Christian movies. Right now I'm making plans to watch 'War Room' because I expect it will give me perspective on how to enhance my prayer life.

As I pressed through to my healing I kept a praise and worship list at hand. This helped me to create the atmosphere to hear from and talk to God. Some of the songs on my list were:

- 10,000 Reasons by Matt Redman
- Already Done by Ryan Mark & Kevin Downswell
- Be Blessed by Yolanda Adams
- Beautiful Day by Jermaine Edwards
- Break Every Chain by Tasha Cobbs
- Daddy Oh by Kerron Ennis & DJ Nicholas
- Every Praise by Hezekiah Walker
- Fill Me Up by Tasha Cobbs
- For Your Glory by Tasha Cobbs
- Freedom by Eddie James
- Good, Good Father by Housefires
- Great Are You Lord by Sinach
- Hallelujah by Jermaine Edwards
- He wants it all by Forever Jones
- I Am A Warrior by Marvia Providence
- I Belong to God by Junior Tucker (Featuring Dawn Martin)
- I Can Only Imagine by Tamela Mann
- I Give You Me by Ripton P Morris
- I Know Who I Am by Sinach
- I Won't Go Back by William McDowell

- Indescribable by Keirra Sheard
- It's Not Over Now by Glacia Robinson
- Jesus At The Center Of At All by Israel Houghton
- Lord I Love You by Adrian Cunningham
- Nobody Greater by Vashawn Mitchell
- Redeemed by Ripton P Morris
- The Anthem by Planetshakers
- Thine Is The Kingdom by Jermaine Gordon
- Things Already Better by Judith Gayle & DJ Nicholas
- Turning Around For Me by Vashawn Mitchell
- You Are God by Jermaine Gordon
- You Make Me Stronger by Kevin Downswell
- Withholding Nothing by William McDowell

In the end, spiritual healing was the starting point for my total turnaround as it spilled over into my family, work, social, and physical life.

My family and social life

Prior to healing I was grouchy, sulky, and suffered from mild depression. I wasn't myself. With healing I became easier to get along with. My brother can attest to the fact that although we still have our issues I snap at him less. I'm more patient. I'm more connected.

There was a point at which I had no social life. I was too ashamed, and perhaps afraid to see people; to be around them. I hated the idea of having to answer questions about my husband, to have to explain what was going on and what went wrong. So I deliberately locked myself away. I found I mostly did school-related things.

With healing I now feel free and that freedom has allowed me to get out, socialize, and fellowship. I'm also part of the board of management of a junior high school, which for me is tremendous as it means I'm giving back to my community.

My work life

Being depressed, suffering from shame, hurt and/or disappointment can cause you to become less focused and can negatively impact your work life. During my relationship I was so hurt by the words and events that I pushed them to the back of my mind, willing myself to forget the painful moments. This of course affected my memory on a whole. It also affected my accuracy, creativity and just general productivity. It affected how well I functioned at work.

With healing I found I went back to being focused. I was now a new and improved me. I was sharper, quicker, and more creative. I also got my memory back which resulted in me exhibiting greater accuracy and productivity.

I felt refreshed. I had more energy than I've ever had and this helped to keep me throughout the day. I now know who I am. Hence I dress, walk, speak and carry myself with purpose. I no longer hold my head down, I no longer feel fear. Rather I feel confident, courageous and every day I look forward to taking on the world.

My physical life

I received physical healing as well. I don't feel as weak as before. I no longer have issues sleeping. I don't feel panicked like before. I actually feel stronger.

My prayer for you is that you'll appreciate the importance of healing, and then take the time and steps to go through the process.

Step 3
Track Your Progress

I had to be sure I was making progress as time passed, so I kept a journal. In my journal I made note of my emotions, thoughts, and actions on a daily basis. I prayed over them, committed them to God asking Him to heal me and to help me maintain that healing.

I was brutally honest as I wrote in my diary. Writing things down made me aware of what was wrong which I then used to determine how I would pray. It made me aware of improvements and of those times when I was slipping back.

In the first few months I noticed that I cried a lot, argued with people a lot, shouted, was on edge, hardly laughed, sometimes even had suicidal thoughts. However, as time passed I saw improvements and that made me feel better about myself. It helped me not to give up hope, because I was able to recognize that there was a silver lining after all.

Truth is, the first few months of writing sounded awful when I read my notes back to myself, and I had to be careful not to be daunted by that. I guess I was able to overcome because the negativity I saw coming up off the pages fueled my prayer life, causing me to cry out to God even more rather than give up hope.

I imagine timelines may differ for each person, but by the third month I was laughing again. By the fifth month I could actually sleep through the night. Not long after that I noticed I was able to go out with friends. Once I got more involved at church and did more voluntary work the sadness and fear dissipated.

Fear stuck with me longer than anything else, but, as I said before, declaring affirmations over my life and believing them helped tremendously.

Here are some of the questions I came up with to help track my progress.

Journal Pages   **Date** _____

The questions below are designed to help you track how you're doing day by day. Be honest with yourself as you complete each one. Do this daily for as long as you need to.

1. What words would you use to describe how you felt for most of today?

a. I was	1 happy	2 sad
b. I wanted to be	1 alive	2 dead
c. I was	1 smiling	2 crying
d. I wanted to be	1 with people	2 alone
e. I wanted to do	1 something fun	2 nothing

2. Describe in as much detail as possible how you would feel if your spouse/other half called you on your mobile phone.

   _____

   _____

3. Describe in as much detail as possible how you would feel if you saw your spouse/other half unexpectedly.

_____

_____

4. What one thing today made you feel better than yesterday and why?

_____

_____

5. What one thing today made you feel worse than yesterday and why?

_____

_____

If you're still dealing with strong feelings of fear, anger, doubt, low self-esteem or any such emotions after making the effort on your own to heal from your hurts and wounds, I encourage you to seek professional and/or spiritual counseling, if you aren't yet doing so.

I also strongly suggest you get help if you're having suicidal thoughts.

Step 4
Avoid Making The Same Mistake

Here are some tips and takeaways to keep in mind when deciding on whether a relationship is right for you.

I attribute these takeaways to Apostle Al Miller who taught on 'Choosing a Partner' at Whole Life College. His teachings opened my eyes and helped me to evaluate my relationship and marriage. His teachings helped me realize that I should have taken the time to get to know myself and my husband, and should have assessed our readiness for marriage.

The following are based on my own experience. They're nuggets I introduced in Part I of this book and thought important to repeat here. Keep them in mind as you move forward after receiving your healing and seek to not make the same mistakes again.

Before marriage
1. Don't spend time alone with a man who is not your husband. Spending time alone may lead to sex which clouds things.

2. Chit-chatting with somebody is not the same as getting to know them.

3. If you have to hide your relationship it may not be of God.

4. Pay attention to signs of aggression such as clenched fists, teeth and others mentioned in Chapter 1.

5. Ask critical questions upfront. Don't assume you share the same vision for life, marriage and parenting.

6. Lust and attraction are not love and will not be enough to survive the challenges of your relationship.

7. Don't use 'signs' as your only guide when making a life changing decision. Spend time planning, evaluating and praying instead.

Marriage
8. Be careful not to get caught up in the euphoria of the wedding without making plans for your marriage.

9. If the people that are closest to you, that you trust most raise a red flag, be wary. It's a good indication that something is wrong.

10. God validates you, not marriage. Knowing this is accepting who God says you are. Not accepting this will negatively affect your marriage.

11. Mushy feelings are not enough to sustain your marriage.

12. Don't buy anything major or get into any contractually binding arrangements together prior to saying "I do", without first giving it serious consideration.

13. How a person is before marriage is an indication of how that person will be during marriage.

14. A man or woman who lacks self-control is not ready yet for marriage.

15. If the relationship isn't working after much effort and counseling maybe you should walk away.

Pregnancy

16. Trapping a man with pregnancy is never a good idea. The decision to have a child should be handled responsibly.

17. Like marriage, pregnancy should be well thought out and planned for.

18. Beware of emotional stress during pregnancy. Ignoring emotional wounds can cause them to deepen and lead to fear and low self-esteem.

19. Getting back together with someone after a traumatic event, for example a miscarriage, is sometimes like starting a relationship on the rebound.

Abuse

20. Take note of how a man treats others including his parents, children, and especially, other women.

21. A man who has to depend on a woman for a protracted period may become aggressive towards her.

22. Be wary if he fluctuates often between being gentle and loving in one instance and aggressive and bullish in the next.

23. A man who responds aggressively when you disagree with him is either suffering from rejection, low self-esteem or is a control freak.

24. Men who abuse women sometimes use suicide to manipulate the women into staying.

25. If you find yourself in an abusive relationship get help. Don't suffer through it alone.

Eyes Wide Open
Adapted. Original version by Ripton P Morris (2007)

He strutted in looking all spruced up and nice
His aim was to separate me from the love of Christ

I smiled to myself, I've been there, I know his type
But my godly diet takes me beyond hoopla and hype

With my 20/20 I saw that his charm was naturally alluring
With the scales removed I found him Spiritually abhorring

He couldn't see GOD's armor so he made his play
But every effort was thwarted by GOD's magnificent array

Oh you sly devil
You…you epitome of evil

Can't you see my eyes are open?
I'm blessed with Kingdom vision

Mine is a Kingdom mission
Don't you know I no longer make my own decision?

Bibliography

Helps Ministries. Helps Word-Studies (2011). Helps Ministries, Inc. Accessed at www.gotquestions.org/dunamis-meaning.html.

How to Recognise Aggression. Accessed at http://www.skillsyouneed.com/ps/dealing-with-aggression2.html

Morris, Rev. Ripton P. Through the Eyes of Love. (Bloomington, IN: Authorhouse, 2007). Available online.

Morris, Rev. Ripton P. Christ Died for Me, Christ Lives In Me. (Charleston, SC: CreateSpace.com, 2010). Available online.

Morris, Rev. Ripton P. Sweet Song (2013). Audio CD. Anointed Words & Music Inc. Available online.

Morris, Rev. Ripton P. Sweeter than Honey: Thought-Provoking Morsels from the Word. (Charleston, SC: CreateSpace.com, 2014). Available online.

Souza, Katie. Healing Your Soul: Real Keys to the Miraculous, Episode 2. Accessed at: https://www.youtube.com/watch?v=7uQaprEnJcg.

Walton, Alice. How Parent's Stress Can Hurt a Child from the Inside Out. Accessed at: http://www.forbes.com/sites/alicegwalton/2012/07/25/how-parents-stress-can-hurt-a-child-from-the-inside-out/.

About the Author

Tricia-Anne Y. Morris is a woman of God, wholly committed to her Christian Faith. She is dedicated to sharing the message of God's Love and believes that life begins only after we've invited God to be our Father, Husband, Way Maker, and Friend.

Tricia-Anne believes in the power of knowing who you are and living your full potential based on Kingdom principles. She says, "I love sharing knowledge with others. Knowledge sharing creates and engenders growth and success. I want to know that people are constantly growing and are being empowered in every area of their lives, in particular, their spiritual, emotional, relational and professional lives. I have a heart for women and young adults and believe I have a duty to help in any way I can by pouring into them, the way others have poured into me."

Over the last 20 years, Tricia-Anne has given back to women and young adults in her capacity as a Mentor and Motivational speaker, spending much of her time helping them in personal and career development. All this, while wearing the hat of a Senior Executive in Research and Business Coach. Her passion for women led her to create the Women Inspiring Prosperity blog community, a space where women can share their disappointments, fears, joys, wins and/or enjoy content that will empower and inspire. Tricia-Anne is also a radio host and Vice President of Anointed Words & Music, Inc. (USA).

Connect with Tricia-Anne via her FB page @triciaanneymorris, her FB group @womeninspiringprosperity, and on twitter @TriciaAnneY. She also invites you to be a part of her blog community at www.womeninspiringprosperity.wordpress.com.

Other Acknowledgements
Huge thanks to the following organizations for all the support given in making this book a reality:

Anointed Words & Music, Inc. (USA)
Fellowship Tabernacle (Jamaica)
Whole Life College (Jamaica)
Whole Life Ministries (Jamaica)
WOGIS Ministries International (Jamaica)

www.ingramcontent.com/pod-product-compliance
Lightning Source LLC
Chambersburg PA
CBHW072202090426
42740CB00012B/2362